GIANT VEHICLES
An Imagination Library Series

GIANT BULLDOZERS

Jim Mezzanotte

GARETH**STEVENS**
GS
PUBLISHING
A Member of the WRC Media Family of Companies

Please visit our web site at: **www.garethstevens.com**
For a free color catalog describing Gareth Stevens Publishing's list of high-quality books
and multimedia programs, call 1-800-542-2595 (USA) or 1-800-387-3178 (Canada).
Gareth Stevens Publishing's fax: (414) 332-3567.

Library of Congress Cataloging-in-Publication Data

Mezzanotte, Jim.
    Giant bulldozers / by Jim Mezzanotte.
      p. cm. — (Giant vehicles)
    Includes bibliographical references and index.
    ISBN 0-8368-4910-8 (lib. bdg.)
    ISBN 0-8368-4917-5 (softcover)
    1. Bulldozers—Juvenile literature. I. Title.
  TA735.M63   2005
  621.8'65—dc22   2005046034

First published in 2006 by
Gareth Stevens Publishing
A Member of the WRC Media Family of Companies
330 West Olive Street, Suite 100
Milwaukee, WI 53212 USA

Editorial direction: Mark J. Sachner
Editor: JoAnn Early Macken
Art direction: Tammy West
Cover design and page layout: Kami M. Koenig
Photo editor: Diane Laska-Swanke
Picture researcher: Martin Levick

Photo credits: Cover, pp. 7, 9, 11, 13, 15, 17, 19, 21 © Eric Orlemann; p. 5 Courtesy of Komatsu America Corp.

Printed in the United States of America

1 2 3 4 5 6 7 8 9 09 08 07 06 05

COVER: A Caterpillar
bulldozer goes to work.

Table of Contents

Words that appear in the glossary are printed in

A Big Push

A giant bulldozer has a simple job. It pushes things. Giant bulldozers—dozers for short—work at **mines** and **quarries**. They help build roads, too. They move dirt, rock, and other things. They can move huge amounts at one time.

To move big loads, giant dozers need a lot of power. They also need good **traction**. Most dozers have **tracks** instead of wheels. The tracks dig into the ground. A giant dozer has a big **blade** in front for pushing.

Dozers have to be tough and reliable. They work long hours in all kinds of weather. People who run dozers are "dozing."

A giant dozer pushes rock and dirt. This dozer is made by Komatsu, a Japanese company.

Dozer History

Early dozers were wood boards. Horses pushed the boards. Crawler **tractors** came out in the early 1900s. They had tracks, not wheels. They were good for pulling and pushing. People put blades on the tractors. The bulldozer was born!

At first, dozers were normal tractors with blades. Then companies made special machines. They were built just to be dozers. The first big dozers came out in the 1950s. But they are small compared to today's dozers. **Engineers** improved the dozers. The dozers kept getting bigger. People wanted big dozers for big jobs. Today, giant dozers do these jobs.

This dozer is the V-Con V220. It was built in the 1970s. It is one of the largest dozers. Only two of these dozers were built.

Tracks or Wheels?

Some dozers have tracks. The tracks are wide belts. Metal squares are linked together like a chain. They make up the belts. The belts have ridges. These ridges dig into the ground. Metal wheels inside the belts make them move. Dozers with tracks are called crawler dozers.

Other dozers have wheels. They are called wheel dozers. Some of the biggest dozers are wheel dozers. They usually work in mines. They get around quicker than crawler dozers. A dozer bends in the middle to make turns. The front and back are on a big hinge.

The LeTourneau company made this wheel dozer. You can see where it bends in the middle. It has stairs for getting to the driver's seat.

How Big Is Big?

A company called Komatsu makes the biggest dozer. It is a crawler dozer. It is called the Super Dozer. The Super Dozer weighs over 150 tons—more than one hundred small cars! Its blade is 25 feet (8 meters) wide—wider than some houses! It is more than twice as tall as most adults. Most cars hold less than 20 gallons (75 liters) of **fuel**. This dozer holds more than 500 gallons (1,900 l) of fuel.

Wheel dozers can be huge, too. Some weigh more than 100 tons. Their wheels are almost twice as tall as most adults. They have ladders for climbing to the cab.

The Komatsu Super Dozer is the biggest dozer in the world. Its huge blade can move just about anything!

Dozer Power

Giant dozers push big loads. They need a lot of power. They have huge **diesel** engines. The engines use diesel fuel, not gasoline. They make over 1,000 **horsepower**—more than four times the power of most cars.

Some wheel dozers have electric motors. Their engines do not turn the wheels. Instead, they make power for the motors. Each wheel has its own motor.

Big **hydraulic** cylinders move the blades. The cylinders are tubes. They have smaller cylinders inside. These tubes are called pistons. The pistons are attached to the blades. Pumps force the oil up inside the cylinder. The oil inside the cylinders pushes the pistons. The pistons slide out, moving the blades.

This dozer's engine makes more than 1,000 horsepower. You can see one of its hydraulic cylinders behind the blade.

In the Cab

Giant dozers work in tough places. But their cabs are very comfortable. The cabs keep out noise. They have heat and **air-conditioning**. Most cabs have seats that ride on a cushion of air. People must sit in dozers for many hours. They are much happier working in a nice cab!

Dozers do not have steering wheels. Instead, they have levers and **joy sticks**. You may have used a joy stick to play a video game. Joy sticks on dozers work the same way. They control where the dozer goes. They control the blade, too. The blade moves up and down. It also tilts to each side.

Inside a dozer cab, there are many controls. But you will not find a steering wheel!

Dozer Jobs

Some giant dozers work on construction sites. They move earth to make the ground level and smooth. When the ground is level, buildings or roads can be built. Many dozers have rippers in the back. The rippers dig up the ground. Other dozers move trash in **landfills**.

Giant dozers also work in pit mines. A pit mine is a big hole. Machines dig for **coal** and other things. Dozers clean up around the digging machines. When the digging is done, it has to be filled back up. Dozers help with this job, too.

This giant dozer is made by Caterpillar. When it is done working, the ground will be level and smooth.

Dozer Makers

Today, only a few companies make giant dozers. Komatsu is one of them. It is a Japanese company. It makes the biggest dozer in the world, the 575-A3 Super Dozer. It makes other big dozers, too.

Caterpillar is a U.S. company. It also makes big dozers. The name comes from an early crawler tractor. That tractor looked like a caterpillar! Over the years, the company has made many dozers. One big dozer is called the D11. Many people have used this dozer for big jobs. The John Deere company also makes big dozers.

Giant dozers cost a lot of money. The Komatsu Super Dozer costs more than one million dollars!

A worker finishes painting a new Caterpillar dozer. Caterpillar makes dozers and other big machines.

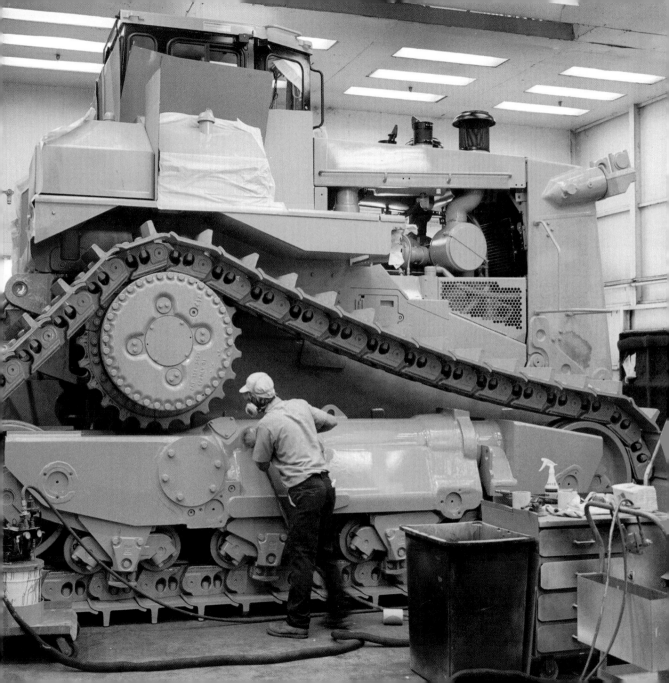

Let's Go Dozing!

Operating a giant dozer takes skill and practice. You cannot see much in front. The blade is in the way. You have to "feel" what the blade pushes. Many people get special training. To learn, they work many hours in dozers. Big dozers can be dangerous. You have to watch for other people. You have to be careful on hills. You could tip over!

It's your turn to operate the dozer. You climb into the cab. You make sure the blade is down. You turn the key, just like in a car. The engine roars. All that power is at your fingertips!

Operating this dozer is a tough job. The big blade makes it hard to see. The dozer will push all that rock and dirt—but you have to be careful!

More to Read and View

Books

Bulldozers. Darlene R. Stille (Compass Point Books)

Bulldozers. Earth Movers (series). Joanne Randolph (PowerKids Press)

Bulldozers. Mighty Machines (series). Linda D. Williams (Pebble Plus)

C Is for Construction: Big Trucks and Diggers from A to Z. Caterpillar
(Chronicle Books)

If I Could Drive A Bulldozer. Tonka (series). Michael Teitelbaum
(Cartwheel)

Look Inside Cross Sections: Bulldozers. Moira Butterfield (DK Publishing)

Videos

Earth Movers (A&E Entertainment)

I Love Big Machines (Consumervision)

I Love Cat Machines (Tapeworm)

There Goes a Bulldozer (A Vision)

Web Sites

Web sites change frequently, but we believe the following web sites are going to last. You can also use good search engines, such as **Yahooligans!** (www.yahooligans.com) or **Google** (www.google.com) to find more information about giant vehicles. Some keywords that will help you are *bulldozers, Caterpillar, construction equipment, crawler dozers, diesel engines, dozers, giant dozers, John Deere,* and *Komatsu.*

auto.howstuffworks.com/
    diesel1.htm
This web site shows how a diesel engine works.

science.howstuffworks.com/
    hydraulic.htm
Visit this web site to learn more about how hydraulic machines work.

www.cat.com/cda/layout?m=
    37840&x=7&location=drop
At this web site, you can see many different Caterpillar machines, including giant dozers. Choose "wheel dozers" or "track-type tractors." Then choose a model by clicking on the model number. You can make the pictures larger. Click on "Benefits & Features" to see more.

www.deere.com/en_US/cfd/
    construction/deere_const/crawlers/
    deere_dozer_selection.html
Visit this web page to see many different John Deere dozers.

www.komatsuamerica.com/index.
    cfm?resource_id=9
The Komatsu web site has many kinds of dozers. Click "dozers" or select it from the list. Then click "specs" to see a picture of each one. You can also enlarge the pictures.

Glossary

You can find these words on the pages listed. Reading a word in a sentence helps you to understand it even better.

air-conditioning (AIR-kun-dish-en-ing): a system that keeps a place cool when it is hot outside. 14

blade (BLAYD): on a bulldozer, the large metal plate on the front that pushes things. 4

coal (KOLE): a black material made of long-dead plants. Coal is a fuel, and it is often used to power electric power plants. 16

engineers (en-jun-EARZ): people who design machines. 6

diesel (DEE-zull): the name for a kind of engine and the special fuel it uses. Most diesel engines are very reliable. They often use less fuel than gas engines. 12

fuel (FYULE): something that burns to provide energy. 10

horsepower (HORS-pow-ur): the amount of power an engine makes, based on how much work one horse can do. 12

hydraulic (hi-DRAW-lick): having to do with using water or another liquid to move something. 12

joy sticks (JOY stiks): levers that move forward and back and from side to side to control a machine. 14

landfills (LAND-filz): places that are built up with layers of trash and soil. 16

mines (MINES): places where coal, gold, silver, and other things are taken out of the ground. Some mines are underground tunnels. Other mines are big holes, or pits. 4

quarries (KWOR-eez): holes in the ground where machines dig up stone, which is used for building things. 4

tracks (TRAX): belts that circle around a row of wheels to move a machine. One wheel in each belt makes it turn. Some tracks are metal plates linked together. Other tracks are loops made of rubber. 4

traction (TRAK-shun): the grip that something has on a surface. To push heavy things, a bulldozer needs a good grip on the ground. 4

tractors (TRAK-turz): vehicles that can pull or push things. 6

Index